CARYL CHU

Caryl Churchill has written for radio. Her stage plays include *Ow.* _ ...~,~. ~~u.. ~ neatre Upstairs, 1972); *Objections to Sex and Violence* (Royal Court, 1975); *Light Shining in Buckinghamshire* (Joint Stock on tour incl. Theatre Upstairs, 1976); *Vinegar Tom* (Monstrous Regiment on tour, incl. Half Moon and ICA, 1976); *Traps* (Theatre Upstairs, 1977), *Cloud Nine* (Joint Stock on tour incl. Royal Court, London, 1979, then Theatre de Lys, New York, 1981); *Three More Sleepless Nights* (Soho Poly and Theatre Upstairs, 1980); *Top Girls* (Royal Court, London, then Public Theater, New York, 1982); *Fen* (Joint Stock on tour, incl. Almeida and Royal Court, London, then Public Theater, New York, 1983); *Softcops* (RSC at the Pit, 1984); *A Mouthful of Birds* with David Lan (Joint Stock on tour, incl. Royal Court, 1986); *Serious Money* (Royal Court and Wyndham's, London, then Public Theater, New York, 1987); *Icecream* (Royal Court, 1989); *Mad Forest* (Central School of Speech and Drama, then Royal Court, 1990); *Lives of the Great Poisoners* with Orlando Gough and Ian Spink (Second Stride on tour, incl. Riverside Studios, London, 1991); *The Skriker* (Royal National Theatre, 1994); *Thyestes* translated from Seneca (Royal Court Theatre Upstairs, 1994); *Hotel* with Orlando Gough and Ian Spink (Second Stride on tour, incl. The Place, London, 1997); *This is a Chair* (London International Festival of Theatre at the Royal Court, 1997); *Blue Heart* (Joint Stock on tour, incl. Royal Court Theatre, 1997); *Far Away* (Royal Court Theatre Upstairs, 2000, and Albery, London, 2001, then New York Theatre Workshop, 2002); *A Number* (Royal Court Theatre, 2002 and the New York Theatre Workshop, 2004).

Plays by Caryl Churchill published by TCG

Blue Heart

Cloud 9

A Dream Play
(adapted from August Strindberg)

Drunk Enough to Say I Love You?

Light Shining in Buckinghamshire

Mad Forest

A Number

The Skriker

This is a Chair

FAR AWAY

Caryl Churchill

THEATRE COMMUNICATIONS GROUP
NEW YORK
2001

TCG books are exclusively distributed to the book trade by Consortium Book Sales and Distribution.

Library of Congress Cataloging-in-Publication Data

Churchill, Caryl.
Far away / by Caryl Churchill.—1st ed.
p. cm.
ISBN 978-1-55936-199-6
1. Social conflict—Drama. I. Title.
2. PR6053.H786F3 2001
3. 822'.914—dc21   2001027317

Cover design by Ned Hoste, 2H.

First TCG Edition, May 2001
Third Printing, March 2008

Far Away was first performed at the Royal Court Theatre Upstairs, London on November 24th, 2000, before transferring to the Abbey Theatre in the West End on January 18th 2001. The cast was as follows:

YOUNG JOAN	Annabelle Seymour-Julen
HARPER	Linda Bassett
TODD	Kevin McKidd
OLDER JOAN	Katherine Tozer

DIRECTOR	Stephen Daldry
DESIGNER	Ian MacNeil
LIGHTING DESIGNER	Rick Fisher
SOUND DESIGNER	Paul Arditti

FAR AWAY

Characters

JOAN, *a girl*

HARPER, *her aunt*

TODD, *a young man*

The Parade (Scene 2.5): five is too few and twenty better than ten. A hundred?

1.

HARPER*'s house. Night.*

JOAN I can't sleep.

HARPER It's the strange bed.

JOAN No, I like different places.

HARPER Are you cold?

JOAN No.

HARPER Do you want a drink?

JOAN I think I am cold.

HARPER That's easy enough then. There's extra blankets in the cupboard.

JOAN Is it late?

HARPER Two.

JOAN Are you going to bed?

HARPER Do you want a hot drink?

JOAN	No thank you.
HARPER	I should go to bed then.
JOAN	Yes.
HARPER	It's always odd in a new place. When you've been here a week you'll look back at tonight and it won't seem the same at all.
JOAN	I've been to a lot of places. I've stayed with friends at their houses. I don't miss my parents if you think that.
HARPER	Do you miss your dog?
JOAN	I miss the cat I think.
HARPER	Does it sleep on your bed?
JOAN	No because I chase it off. But it gets in if the door's not properly shut. You think you've shut the door but it hasn't caught and she pushes it open in the night.
HARPER	Come here a minute. You're shivering. Are you hot?
JOAN	No, I'm all right.
HARPER	You're over-tired. Go to bed. I'm going to bed myself.

JOAN   I went out.

HARPER   When? just now?

JOAN   Just now.

HARPER   No wonder you're cold. It's hot in the
              daytime here but it's cold at night.

JOAN   The stars are brighter here than at
              home.

HARPER   It's because there's no street lights.

JOAN   I couldn't see much.

HARPER   I don't expect you could. How did you
              get out? I didn't hear the door.

JOAN   I went out the window.

HARPER   I'm not sure I like that.

JOAN   No it's quite safe, there's a roof and a
              tree.

HARPER   When people go to bed they should stay
              in bed. Do you climb out of the window
              at home?

JOAN   I can't at home because - No I don't.

HARPER   I'm responsible for you.

JOAN   Yes, I'm sorry.

HARPER   Well that's enough adventures for one
            night. You'll sleep now. Off you go. Look
            at you, you're asleep on your feet.

JOAN   There was a reason.

HARPER   For going out?

JOAN   I heard a noise.

HARPER   An owl?

JOAN   A shriek.

HARPER   An owl then. There are all sorts of
            birds here, you might see a golden
            oriole. People come here specially to
            watch birds and we sometimes make
            tea or coffee or sell bottles of water
            because there's no café and people
            don't expect that and they get thirsty.
            You'll see in the morning what a
            beautiful place it is.

JOAN   It was more like a person screaming.

HARPER   It is like a person screaming when you
            hear an owl.

JOAN   It was a person screaming.

HARPER   Poor girl, what a fright you must have
           had imagining you heard somebody
           screaming. You should have come
           straight down here to me.

JOAN   I wanted to see.

HARPER   It was dark.

JOAN   Yes but I did see.

HARPER   Now what did you imagine you saw in
           the dark?

JOAN   I saw my uncle.

HARPER   Yes I expect you did. He likes a breath of
           air. He wasn't screaming I hope?

JOAN   No.

HARPER   That's all right then. Did you talk to
           him? I expect you were frightened he'd
           say what are you doing out of your bed
           so late.

JOAN   I stayed in the tree.

HARPER   He didn't see you?

JOAN   No.

HARPER   He'll be surprised won't he, he'll laugh
           when he hears you were up in the tree.
           He'll be cross but he doesn't mean it,

he'll think it's a good joke, it's the sort of thing he did when he was a boy. So bed now. I'll go up too.

JOAN   He was pushing someone. He was bundling someone into a shed.

HARPER   He must have been putting a big sack in the shed. He works too late.

JOAN   I'm not sure if it was a woman. It could have been a young man.

HARPER   Well I have to tell you, when you've been married as long as I have. There are things people get up to, it's natural, it's nothing bad, that's just friends of his your uncle was having a little party with.

JOAN   Was it a party?

HARPER   Just a little party.

JOAN   Yes because there wasn't just that one person.

HARPER   No, there'd be a few of his friends.

JOAN   There was a lorry.

HARPER   Yes, I expect there was.

JOAN   When I put my ear against the side of the lorry I heard crying inside.

HARPER   How could you do that from up in the tree?

JOAN   I got down from the tree. I went to the lorry after I looked in the window of the shed.

HARPER   There might be things that are not your business when you're a visitor in someone else's house.

JOAN   Yes, I'd rather not have seen. I'm sorry.

HARPER   Nobody saw you?

JOAN   They were thinking about themselves.

HARPER   I think it's lucky nobody saw you.

JOAN   If it's a party, why was there so much blood?

HARPER   There isn't any blood.

JOAN   Yes.

HARPER   Where?

JOAN   On the ground.

HARPER   In the dark? how would you see that in
           the dark?

JOAN   I slipped in it.

           She holds up her bare foot.

           I mostly wiped it off.

HARPER   That's where the dog got run over this
           afternoon.

JOAN   Wouldn't it have dried up?

HARPER   Not if the ground was muddy.

JOAN   What sort of dog?

HARPER   A big dog, a big mongrel.

JOAN   That's awful, you must be very sad, had
           you had him long?

HARPER   No, he was young, he ran out, he was
           never very obedient, a lorry was backing
           up.

JOAN   What was his name?

HARPER   Flash.

JOAN   What colour was he?

HARPER   Black with a bit of white.

JOAN   Why were the children in the shed?

HARPER   What children?

JOAN   Don't you know what children?

HARPER   How could you see there were children?

JOAN   There was a light on. That's how I
            could see the blood inside the shed. I
            could see the faces and which ones had
            blood on.

HARPER   You've found out something secret. You
            know that don't you?

JOAN   Yes.

HARPER   Something you shouldn't know.

JOAN   Yes I'm sorry.

HARPER   Something you must never talk about.
            Because if you do you could put people's
            lives in danger.

JOAN   Why? who from? from my uncle?

HARPER   Of course not from your uncle.

JOAN   From you?

HARPER	Of course not from me, are you mad? I'm going to tell you what's going on. Your uncle is helping these people. He's helping them escape. He's giving them shelter. Some of them were still in the lorry, that's why they were crying. Your uncle's going to take them all into the shed and then they'll be all right.
JOAN	They had blood on their faces.
HARPER	That's from before. That's because they were attacked by the people your uncle's saving them from.
JOAN	There was blood on the ground.
HARPER	One of them was injured very badly but your uncle bandaged him up.
JOAN	He's helping them.
HARPER	That's right.
JOAN	There wasn't a dog. There wasn't a party.
HARPER	No, I'm trusting you with the truth now. You must never talk about it or you'll put your uncle's life in danger and mine and even your own. You won't even say anything to your parents.

JOAN	Why did you have me to stay if you've got this secret going on?
HARPER	The lorry should have come yesterday. It won't happen again while you're here.
JOAN	It can now because I know. You don't have to stop for me. I could help uncle in the shed and look after them.
HARPER	No, he has to do it himself. But thank you for offering, that's very kind. So after all that excitement do you think you could go back to bed?
JOAN	Why was uncle hitting them?
HARPER	Hitting who?
JOAN	He was hitting a man with a stick. I think the stick was metal. He hit one of the children.
HARPER	One of the people in the lorry was a traitor. He wasn't really one of them, he was pretending, he was going to betray them, they found out and told your uncle. Then he attacked your uncle, he attacked the other people, your uncle had to fight him.

JOAN   That's why there was so much blood.

HARPER   Yes, it had to be done to save the
            others.

JOAN   He hit one of the children.

HARPER   That would have been the child of the
            traitor. Or sometimes you get bad
            children who even betray their parents.

JOAN   What's going to happen?

HARPER   They'll go off in the lorry very early in
            the morning.

JOAN   Where to?

HARPER   Where they're escaping to. You don't
            want to have to keep any more secrets.

JOAN   He only hit the traitors.

HARPER   Of course. I'm not surprised you can't
            sleep, what an upsetting thing to see.
            But now you understand, it's not so
            bad. You're part of a big movement
            now to make things better. You can be
            proud of that. You can look at the stars
            and think here we are in our little bit
            of space, and I'm on the side of the
            people who are putting things right,

and your soul will expand right into the
sky.

JOAN   Can't I help?

HARPER   You can help me clean up in the
              morning. Will you do that?

JOAN   Yes.

HARPER   So you'd better get some sleep.

2.

Several years later. A hat makers.

1.

JOAN *and* TODD *are sitting at a workbench. They have each just started making a hat.*

TODD There's plenty of blue.

JOAN I think I'm starting with black.

TODD Colour always wins.

JOAN I will have colour, I'm starting with black to set the colour off.

TODD I did one last week that was an abstract picture of the street, blue for the buses, yellow for the flats, red for the leaves, grey for the sky. Nobody got it but I knew what it was. There's little satisfactions to be had.

JOAN Don't you enjoy it?

TODD You're new aren't you?

JOAN	This is my first hat. My first professional hat.
TODD	Did you do hat at college?
JOAN	My degree hat was a giraffe six feet tall.
TODD	You won't have time to do something like that in the week.
JOAN	I know.
TODD	We used to get two weeks before a parade and then they took it down to one and now they're talking about cutting a day.
JOAN	So we'd get an extra day off?
TODD	We'd get a day's less money. We wouldn't make such good hats.
JOAN	Can they do that?
TODD	You'd oppose it would you?
JOAN	I've only just started.
TODD	You'll find there's a lot wrong with this place.
JOAN	I thought it was one of the best jobs.

TODD   It is. Do you know where to go for
          lunch?

JOAN   I think there's a canteen isn't there?

TODD   Yes but we don't go there. I'll show you
          where to go.

2.

Next day. They are working on the hats, which are by now far more brightly decorated ie the ones they were working on have been replaced by ones nearer completion.

JOAN   Your turn.

TODD   I go for a swim in the river before
          work.

JOAN   Isn't it dangerous?

TODD   Your turn.

JOAN   I've got a pilot's licence.

TODD   I stay up till four every morning
          watching the trials.

JOAN	I'm getting a room in a subway.
TODD	I've got my own place.
JOAN	Have you?
TODD	Do you want to see it? That's coming on.
JOAN	I don't understand yours but I like the feather.
TODD	I'm not trying. I've been here too long.
JOAN	Will you leave?
TODD	My turn. There's something wrong with how we get the contracts.
JOAN	But we want the contracts.
TODD	What if we don't deserve them? What if our work isn't really the best?
JOAN	So what's going on?
TODD	I'll just say a certain person's brother-in-law. Where does he work do you think?
JOAN	Where does he work?
TODD	I'm not talking about it in here. Tell me something else.

JOAN   I don't like staying in in the evenings and
                watching trials.

TODD   I watch them at night after I come back.

JOAN   Back from where?

TODD   Where do you like?

3.

Next day. They're working on the hats, which are getting very big and extravagant.

TODD   I don't enjoy animal hats myself.

JOAN   I was a student.

TODD   Abstract hats are back in a big way.

JOAN   I've always liked abstract hats.

TODD   You must have not noticed when
                everyone hated them.

JOAN   It was probably before my time.

                Silence. They go on working.

JOAN   It's just if you're going on about it all the
               time I don't know why you don't do
               something about it.

TODD   This is your third day.

JOAN   The management's corrupt – you've told
               me. We're too low paid – you've told me.

               Silence. They go on working.

TODD   Too much green.

JOAN   It's meant to be too much.

               Silence. They go on working.

TODD   I noticed you looking at that fair boy's
               hat. I hope you told him it was
               derivative.

               Silence. They go on working.

TODD   I'm the only person in this place who's
               got any principles, don't tell me I should
               do something, I spend my days
               wondering what to do.

JOAN   So you'll probably come up with
               something.

               Silence. They go on working.

4.

*Next day. They are working on the hats, which are now enormous
and preposterous.*

TODD	That's beautiful.
JOAN	You like it?
TODD	I do.
JOAN	I like yours too.
TODD	You don't have to say that. It's not one of my best.
JOAN	No it's got - I don't know, it's a confident hat.
TODD	I have been doing parades for six years. So I'm a valued old hand. So when I go and speak to a certain person he might pay attention.
JOAN	You're going to speak to him?
TODD	I've an appointment after work.
JOAN	You might lose your job.

TODD   I might.

JOAN   I'm impressed.

TODD   That was the idea.

JOAN   Will you mention the brother-in-law?

TODD   First I'll talk about the money. Then I'll just touch in the brother-in-law. I've a friend who's a journalist.

JOAN   Will you touch in the journalist?

TODD   I might imply something without giving the journalist away. It might be better if he can't trace the journalist back to me.

JOAN   Though he will suspect.

TODD   However much he suspects. One thing if I lost my job.

JOAN   What's that?

TODD   I'd miss you.

JOAN   Already?

5.

Next day. A procession of ragged, beaten, chained prisoners, each wearing a hat, on their way to execution. The finished hats are even more enormous and preposterous than in the previous scene.

6.

A new week. JOAN *and* TODD *are starting work on new hats.*

JOAN   I still can't believe it.

TODD   No one's ever won in their first week before.

JOAN   It's all going to be downhill from now on.

TODD   You can't win every week.

JOAN   That's what I mean.

TODD   No but you'll do a fantastic body of work while you're here.

JOAN   Sometimes I think it's a pity that more aren't kept.

TODD   There'd be too many, what would they do with them?

JOAN   They could reuse them.

TODD   Exactly and then we'd be out of work.

JOAN   It seems so sad to burn them with the bodies.

TODD   No I think that's the joy of it. The hats are ephemeral. It's like a metaphor for something or other.

JOAN   Well, life.

TODD   Well, life, there you are. Out of nearly three hundred hats I've made here I've only had three win and go in the museum. But that's never bothered me. You make beauty and it disappears, I love that.

JOAN   You're so..

TODD   What?

JOAN   You make me think in different ways.
                Like I'd never have thought about how
                this place is run and now I see how
                important it is.

TODD   I think it did impress a certain person
                that I was speaking from the high moral
                ground.

JOAN   So tell me again exactly what he said at
                the end.

TODD   "These things must be thought about."

JOAN   I think that's encouraging.

TODD   It could mean he'll think how to get rid
                of me.

JOAN   That's a fantastic shape to start from.

TODD   It's a new one for me. I'm getting
                inspired by you.

JOAN   There's still the journalist. If he looks
                into it a bit more we could expose the
                corrupt financial basis of how the whole
                hat industry is run, not just this place,
                I bet the whole industry is dodgy.

TODD   Do you think so?

JOAN   I think we should find out.

TODD   You've changed my life, do you know
            that?

JOAN   If you lose your job I'll resign.

TODD   We might not get jobs in hats again.

JOAN   There's other parades.

TODD   But I think you're a hat genius.

JOAN   Unless all the parades are corrupt.

TODD   I love these beads. Use these beads.

JOAN   No, you have them.

TODD   No, you.

3.

Several years later. HARPER*'s house, daytime.*

HARPER   You were right to poison the wasps.

TODD   Yes, I think all the wasps have got to
            go.

HARPER   I was outside yesterday on the edge of
            the wood when a shadow came over
            and it was a cloud of butterflies, and
            they came down just beyond me and
            the trees and bushes were red with
            them. Two of them clung to my arm,
            I was terrified, one of them got in my
            hair, I managed to squash them.

TODD   I haven't had a problem with
            butterflies.

HARPER   They can cover your face. The Romans
            used to commit suicide with gold leaf,
            just flip it down their throat and it
            covered their windpipe, I think of that
            with butterflies.

TODD   I was passing an orchard, there were
            horses standing under the trees, and
            suddenly wasps attacked them out of the
            plums. There were the horses galloping
            by screaming with their heads made of
            wasp. I wish she'd wake up.

HARPER   We don't know how long she'd been
            walking.

TODD   She was right to come.

HARPER   You don't go walking off in the middle of
            a war.

TODD   You do if you're escaping.

HARPER   We don't know that she was escaping.

TODD   She was getting to a place of safety to
            regroup.

HARPER   Is this a place of safety?

TODD   Relatively, yes of course it is. Everyone
            thinks it's just a house.

HARPER   The cats have come in on the side of the
            French.

TODD   I never liked cats, they smell, they
            scratch, they only like you because you
            feed them, they bite, I used to have a

cat that would suddenly just take some bit of you in its mouth.

HARPER   Did you know they've been killing babies?

TODD   Where's that?

HARPER   In China. They jump in the cots when nobody's looking.

TODD   But some cats are still ok.

HARPER   I don't think so.

TODD   I know a cat up the road.

HARPER   No, you must be careful of that.

TODD   But we're not exactly on the other side from the French. It's not as if they're the Moroccans and the ants.

HARPER   It's not as if they're the Canadians, the Venezuelans and the mosquitoes.

TODD   It's not as if they're the engineers, the chefs, the children under five, the musicians.

HARPER   The car salesmen.

TODD   Portuguese car salesmen.

HARPER   Russian swimmers.

TODD   Thai butchers.

HARPER   Latvian dentists.

TODD   No, the Latvian dentists have been doing
           good work in Cuba. They've a house
           outside Havana.

HARPER   But Latvia has been sending pigs to
           Sweden. The dentists are linked to
           international dentistry and that's where
           their loyalty lies, with dentists in Dar-es-
           Salaam.

TODD   We don't argue about Dar-es-Salaam.

HARPER   You would attempt to justify the
           massacre in Dar-es-Salaam?

           She's come here because you're here on
           leave and if anyone finds out I'll be held
           responsible.

TODD   It's only till tomorrow. I'll wake her up.
           I'll give her a few more minutes.

HARPER   Did you see the programme about
           crocodiles?

TODD   Yes but crocodiles, the way they look
           after the baby crocodiles and carry

them down to the water in their
mouths.

HARPER   Don't you think everyone helps their own
children?

TODD   I'm just saying I wouldn't be sorry if
the crocodiles were on one of the sides
we have alliances with. They're
unstoppable, come on.

HARPER   Crocodiles are evil and it is always right
to be opposed to crocodiles. Their
skin, their teeth, the foul smell of their
mouths from the dead meat. Crocodiles
wait till zebras are crossing the river
and bite the weak ones with those
jaws and pull them down. Crocodiles
invade villages at night and take
children out of their beds. A crocodile
will carry a dozen heads back to the
river, tenderly like it carries its young,
and put them in the water where they
bob about as trophies till they rot.

TODD   I'm just saying we could use that.

HARPER   And the fluffy little darling waterbirds,
the smallest one left behind squeaking
wait for me, wait for me. And their
mother who would give her life to save
them.

TODD   Do we include mallards in this?

HARPER   Mallards are not a good waterbird. They
              commit rape, and they're on the side of
              the elephants and the Koreans. But
              crocodiles are always in the wrong.

TODD   Do you think I should wake her up or let
              her sleep? We won't get any time
              together.

HARPER   You agree with me about the crocodiles?

TODD   What's the matter? you don't know
              whose side I'm on?

HARPER   I don't know what you think.

TODD   I think what we all think.

HARPER   Take deer.

TODD   You mean sweet little bambis?

HARPER   You mean that ironically?

TODD   I mean it sarcastically.

HARPER   Because they burst out of parks and
              storm down from mountains and
              terrorise shopping malls. If the does run
              away when you shoot they run into
              somebody else and trample them with

their vicious little shining hooves, the
fawns get under the feet of shoppers and
send them crashing down escalators, the
young bucks charge the plate glass
windows –

TODD   I know to hate deer.

HARPER   and the old ones, do you know how
            heavy their antlers are or how sharp the
            prongs are when they twist into teenagers
            running down the street?

TODD   Yes I do know that.

            He lifts his shirt and shows a scar.

HARPER   Was that a deer?

TODD   In fact it was a bear. I don't like being
            doubted.

HARPER   It was when the elephants went over to
            the Dutch, I'd always trusted elephants.

TODD   I've shot cattle and children in Ethiopia.
            I've gassed mixed troops of Spanish,
            computer programmers and dogs. I've
            torn starlings apart with my bare hands.
            And I liked doing it with my bare hands.
            So don't suggest I'm not reliable.

HARPER   I'm not saying you can't kill.

TODD   And I know it's not all about excitement.
            I've done boring jobs. I've worked in
            abattoirs stunning pigs and musicians
            and by the end of the day your back
            aches and all you can see when you shut
            your eyes is people hanging upside down
            by their feet.

HARPER   So you'd say the deer are vicious?

TODD   We've been over that.

HARPER   If a hungry deer came into the yard you
            wouldn't feed it?

TODD   Of course not.

HARPER   I don't understand that because the deer
            are with us. They have been for three
            weeks.

TODD   I didn't know. You said yourself.

HARPER   Their natural goodness has come
            through. You can see it in their soft
            brown eyes.

TODD   That's good news.

HARPER   You hate the deer. You admire the
            crocodiles.

TODD   I've lost touch because I'm tired.

HARPER   You must leave.

TODD   I'm your family.

HARPER   Do you think I sleep?

              JOAN *comes in and walks into* TODD*'s*
              arms.

HARPER   You can't stay here, they'll be after you.
              What are you going to say when you go
              back, you ran off to spend a day with
              your husband? Everyone has people they
              love they'd like to see or anyway people
              they'd rather see than lie in a hollow
              waiting to be bitten by ants. Are you not
              going back at all because if you're not
              you might as well shoot me now. Did
              anyone see you leave? which way did you
              come? were you followed? There are
              ospreys here who will have seen you
              arrive. And you're risking your life for
              you don't know what because he says
              things that aren't right. Don't you care?
              Maybe you don't know right from wrong
              yourself, what do I know about you after
              two years, I'd like to be glad to see you
              but how can I?

JOAN   Of course birds saw me, everyone saw
              me walking along but nobody knew why,
              I could have been on a mission,

everyone's moving about and no one
knows why, and in fact I killed two cats
and a child under five so it wasn't that
different from a mission, and I don't see
why I can't have one day and then go
back, I'll go on to the end after this. It
wasn't so much the birds I was frightened
of, it was the weather, the weather here's
on the side of the Japanese. There were
thunderstorms all through the
mountains, I went through towns I
hadn't been before. The rats are bleeding
out of their mouths and ears, which is
good, and so were the girls by the side of
the road. It was tiring there because
everything's been recruited, there were
piles of bodies and if you stopped to find
out there was one killed by coffee or one
killed by pins, they were killed by heroin,
petrol, chainsaws, hairspray, bleach,
foxgloves, the smell of smoke was where
we were burning the grass that wouldn't
serve. The Bolivians are working with
gravity, that's a secret so as not to spread
alarm. But we're getting further with
noise and there's thousands dead of light
in Madagascar. Who's going to mobilise
darkness and silence? that's what I
wondered in the night. By the third day
I could hardly walk but I got down to the

river. There was a camp of Chilean
soldiers upstream but they hadn't seen
me and fourteen black and white cows
downstream having a drink so I knew I'd
have to go straight across. But I didn't
know whose side the river was on, it
might help me swim or it might drown
me. In the middle the current was
running much faster, the water was
brown, I didn't know if that meant
anything. I stood on the bank a long
time. But I knew it was my only way of
getting here so at last I put one foot in
the river. It was very cold but so far that
was all. When you've just stepped in you
can't tell what's going to happen. The
water laps round your ankles in any case.